Letters To Parents

Letters To Parents

Grades 1—6

OVER 200 Ideas for Building Reading Skills

Anthony D. Fredericks, Ed.D.
Elaine Papandrea LeBlanc, Ph.D.

Scott, Foresman and Company

Glenview, Illinois   London

To my parents, who gave me doors to
open and dreams to share. —A.D.F.

To my husband, Richard, and my
daughter, Christina, who made the dream
of parenthood a pleasant reality. —E.P.L.

ISBN 0-673-18279-7

14 15 - MAL - 96 95

PREFACE

Educators know the importance of parental involvement in a student's reading growth. Parents can be a vital factor in guiding a child's intellectual development as well as providing the foundation for successful school experiences in reading. Educators are also aware that a day has only so many hours in it. Teachers often don't have the extra time needed to create special materials for parents to use with their children.

This book helps solve that problem by providing dozens of carefully prepared letters for parents that teachers can send home weekly. Each of the forty letters focuses on direct and easy-to-implement reading activities that can be incorporated regularly into the family's daily routine without turning the home into a "school away from school." The suggestions and tips are all proven methods for developing and encouraging successful and responsible readers.

Written in easy-to-understand language, *Letters to Parents* gives both parents and teachers scores of additional ideas to encourage positive and regular communication between home and school. These letters are suitable for gifted, developmental, or remedial students and are not tied to any specific grade level. They are also compatible to any reading series since they emphasize basic skills appropriate for any elementary child. All in all, the book is a convenient, ready reference for any teacher seeking to involve parents in the educational process.

CONTENTS

Special Energizers

Award Certificate

HOW TO USE THIS BOOK

This book is designed to help you stimulate greater reading achievement for your students through an active partnership with their parents. Each of the letters and activities has been selected after a careful evaluation of the reading needs of most children as well as the requests of many parents. The letters are intended to encourage children and parents to work together for reading success in a relaxed manner within their family situation.

There are forty letters in all. They are organized into fifteen high interest categories with two or three letters in each category. One category, "Information Please," includes an introductory letter and an evaluation letter. The latter can be used at various times during the year.

Starting at the beginning of the school year, you are encouraged to send home these letters to the parents on a weekly basis. The following procedure is suggested:

1. Photocopy one letter and sign your name in the space provided at the bottom of the letter. Be sure to add the date at the top of the letter.

2. Photocopy the letter in a quantity sufficient for each student in your class.

3. Send the letter home with your students on a selected day of each week (Mondays, for example).

4. Encourage students to work with their parents on the activities and projects listed in individual letters. Emphasize that these are not "homework" assignments, but rather an opportunity for families to work together.

5. You may wish to encourage students to bring in some of their home projects to share with other members of the class. Point out that no grades will be assigned or recorded.

Alternate Strategies

The following strategies may help to facilitate a two-way communication of the letters between home and school:

1. Include a letter as part of a regular newsletter/newspaper sent home by the school or prepared by your students.

2. Clip the letters to regular classwork or homework papers sent home weekly to parents.

3. Write a brief, personalized note at the bottom of each letter commenting on something positive about the student.

4. Schedule regular workshops at school throughout the year at which parents can share their favorite home reading activities. Be sure to share some additional reading activities as well.

5. Ask the principal or superintendent to prepare a special introductory letter to parents explaining the letters and suggesting an end-of-the-year surprise for participating families. Attach the first parent letter.

There are many more ways that you can use to distribute these letters to parents. Encourage your students to suggest alternate methods for getting the letters home.

Special Features

In addition to these letters, this book contains several other features which will make your job easier. The first category, "Information Please," includes an INTRODUCTORY LETTER which explains to parents the importance of their involvement in their child's reading. You may want to send this letter home during the first weeks of school.

An additional feature included in this first category is an EVALUATION LETTER which is designed to enable parents to react to the letters which you have sent home. You may want to send this letter home with regular school progress reports.

The third feature is a SKILLS ORGANIZATION CHART. This chart will enable you to coordinate the letters with the following skill areas: word attack, vocabulary, comprehension, and study skills. This chart can be found on page xii.

The fourth feature is a set of SPECIAL ENERGIZERS. These sheets will allow you to provide supportive reading activities as well as more specific information on developing positive reading habits.

The final special feature of this book is the AWARD CERTIFICATE. This certificate, signed by the appropriate officials (including you), can be distributed at an end-of-the-year ceremony. The ceremony could be part of a special event such as a parents' night, a school picnic, an awards dinner, or a class party.

SKILL ORGANIZATION CHART

These letters are not organized into a rigid pattern. Consequently, teachers can send letters home in any order which blends with their reading program or satisfies the needs of their pupils. You are encouraged, however, to send the letters home on a once-a-week basis throughout the year to achieve maximum results.

Teachers interested in correlating general reading skills within these letters with other reading materials may find the following chart to be appropriate. It lists the individual letter titles down the left hand side of the chart and general skill areas across the top of the chart. Bullets are then positioned within the chart according to the skill areas emphasized in each letter. This format allows you to individualize your letter selection. For example, if you wanted to send home letters reinforcing comprehension skills you could select some from the third column. At the same time, there may be other students who need extra support in the area of vocabulary. Several letters could be chosen from the second column. This process allows you to select the letters most appropriate to individual needs.

NOTE: You may find it helpful to duplicate multiple copies of each letter as well as the SPECIAL ENERGIZERS at the beginning of the school year and place them in a three-ring binder. As individual needs arise, you can then select materials in a quick and convenient manner.

SKILL ORGANIZATION CHART

	WORD ATTACK	VOCABULARY	COMPREHENSION	STUDY SKILLS
1. Introductory Letter				
2. Evaluation Letter				
3. Sharing Reading Time		●	●	●
4. Reading Aloud with Your Child			●	
5. Making Reading Fun			●	●
6. Motivating Your Child through Television			●	
7. Family Reading Activities		●		●
8. Setting a Good Example				●
9. Providing Encouragement		●		●
10. Building Positive Attitudes	●			
11. Selecting Books with Your Child			●	
12. Children's Interests			●	
13. Selecting Books for Your Child: Resources			●	●
14. Developing Good Comprehension			●	●
15. Comprehension Hints			●	
16. More Comprehension Ideas		●	●	
17. The Importance of Questions			●	
18. Story Questions			●	
19. Asking Everyday Questions			●	●
20. Vocabulary Growth		●		
21. Learning New Words		●		
22. A Strong Vocabulary		●		●
23. Reading and Writing				●
24. Writing at Home		●	●	●
25. Providing Many Experiences		●	●	
26. Learning from Experiences		●		
27. Experiences Lead to Reading		●	●	●
28. Using Children's Magazines			●	
29. Children's Book Clubs		●	●	
30. In the Public Library			●	
31. Public Library Services	●			
32. Using the Newspaper			●	●
33. Newspaper Activities	●	●		●
34. Newspaper Fun	●	●	●	
35. Information Agencies			●	●
36. Special Parent Brochures		●		
37. Free Book Lists			●	●
38. Winter Vacation Activities		●		
39. Spring Vacation Activities		●		●
40. Summer Vacation Activities	●	●	●	●

Parent
Letters

Dear Parents,

Our class will be studying many new ideas in reading this year. Students will be learning word meanings and how to comprehend more of what they read. All of the reading lessons will be filled with exciting stories and lots of valuable learning experiences.

I would like to invite you to become a partner in your child's learning experiences in reading this year. I believe your involvement will help your child attain a higher level of reading success. This partnership between home and school can provide your child with a wealth of learning opportunities that will last a lifetime.

In order to help reinforce the work we are doing in the classroom, I will be sending home prepared parent letters regularly with activities for you and your child to share. These letters are designed to provide you with ideas that can help your child become the best reader possible. Each letter contains several choices of activities to share -- activities that will reinforce your child's reading habit without disrupting your schedule. There are no special materials to buy, no expensive equipment nor electronic do-dads. Your only investment is a few moments of your time each day -- a few moments that can make a world of difference in your child's education.

I look forward to your participation in our reading experiences this year. If you have any questions about these letters or activities, please feel free to contact me. Let's work together this year to help your child succeed in reading!

Sincerely,

EVALUATION LETTER # _____

Dear Parents,

　　For the last several weeks you and your child have shared the Parent Reading Letters portion of our classroom reading program. As you know, these letters have been sent home to help you share ideas that reinforce skills taught in the classroom.

　　I am very interested in learning about your reaction to these letters. Your ideas will help me understand your child better so that I might be able to provide you with additional ideas. Will you please take a few moments of your time to complete the items below and have your child return this form to school? Thanks for your interest and participation!

Sincerely,

My child and I found the reading letters to be: (check one)

　　_____ Very interesting

　　_____ Good

　　_____ Average

　　_____ Not interesting

Comments:

I would like to receive additional reading materials to use at home.

　　_____ Yes　　　　　　　　　　　_____ No

_____　　　_____
Signature of parent/guardian　　　　　Date

SHARING READING TIME

Dear Parents,

Reading stories to your children is a most valuable activity. When children listen to adults read, it helps them develop an appreciation for written material and for the ideas and thoughts that books can convey. Many experts in the field of reading have determined that parents who read to their children on a regular basis are more likely to have children who are good readers.

Reading aloud is perhaps the most important way you can guide your child toward reading success. You can open up whole new worlds of adventure and mystery that cannot be found anywhere else, including TV! Children who have been read to will undoubtedly be eager to read for themselves because they know of the pleasures to be found in books. Here are some suggestions.

1. Before reading to your child, practice reading aloud by yourself the first few times to feel more comfortable.

2. Establish a relaxed atmosphere with no radios, TV, or other distractions. Try setting aside a family reading time when everyone reads.

3. Encourage your child to stop you to ask questions or to point out details. This shows that your child is interested in what you are reading.

4. You may want to stop from time to time in your reading to ask questions about some of the characters or events in the story. Ask questions like "Why do you think he/she did that?"

5. As you read a story, record it on cassette tape. Later, your child can listen to the story again just by playing the tape independently.

READING "SPARKLER" OF THE WEEK: Help your child create a personal bookmark for use in his or her books. Put a wallet-size photo of your child or family between two pieces of clear Contac paper. Then sprinkle in some glitter or colored confetti, seal, and cut to size. Your child may want to make personalized bookmarks for other members of the family, too.

Sincerely,

READING ALOUD WITH YOUR CHILD

Dear Parents,

    Learning to read is one of the most valuable skills your child will ever learn. One practice that helps children continue on the road to reading success is for parents to set aside a special time each day to read with their children. This sharing time is important since it demonstrates to your child that reading can be fun, exciting, and informative. Best of all, when parents and children read together they have a special sharing time -- available in no other activity. This time together not only helps your child develop a positive relationship toward books, but also reinforces the important emotional bond between parent and child. Plan to take a few moments each day to share the joy of literature with your child. Here are some ideas.

1. Give your child plenty of opportunities to choose the reading materials you read together. Let him or her pick books based on special interests or hobbies.

2. Read aloud with lots of expression. You may wish to take on the role of one of the characters in a book and adjust your voice accordingly.

3. As you read an old familiar story to your child, occasionally leave out a word and ask your child to supply the missing word or synonym.

4. Every once in a while do some shared reading. You read one paragraph to your child and your child reads one paragraph to you.

5. Make reading a regular part of your family activities. Be sure to take books along on family outings or trips. Read to your child every chance you get.

READING "SPARKLER" OF THE WEEK: Cut out words from newspaper headlines and place them in a small bag. Ask your child to reach in the bag and select a word. Direct him or her to use the word in a sentence. Write these sentences and post them on the refrigerator or family bulletin board. Older children may wish to select sentences from the newspaper that have been cut out and put in a box. Each sentence can be used in an original story created by your youngster.

Sincerely,

MAKING READING FUN

Dear Parents,

     In order for children to enjoy reading and make it a significant part
of their lives, they must be motivated to explore new books and stories.
We know that children who are motivated to read are children who will want
to read. One way that children become motivated to read is when they are
provided with opportunities to become more involved in the reading process.
When children feel that they are a part of the action or can relate the
action to their own personal experiences, they will develop a very positive
attitude toward their own reading development. Try these motivators.

1. Help your child set up his or her own home library system. Ask
    your child for possible categories of books (i.e. scarey books,
    fun books, action books). Make up signs and post them over the
    family bookcase.

2. Ask your child to make up "reviews" of some of his or her books.
    Write these on separate index cards and keep them in a file box.
    When your child is unsure of a book to read, a quick check through
    the box may locate an old favorite.

3. Help your child write letters to some prominent people in your
    town or community (mayor, sports figure). Ask them about their
    favorite books and why they enjoyed them. This may be a stimulus
    for your child to read them, too.

4. Take lots of photographs of your child reading either alone or
    with someone else. Paste these on sheets of paper and ask your
    child to suggest titles for each one. Then display them.

5. After you and your child finish reading a book together, create a
    puppet or model of one of the characters. These can be displayed
    on top of a bookcase.

READING "SPARKLER" OF THE WEEK: After you and your child have finished
reading a book together, encourage your child to draw new illustrations on
separate sheets of paper. He or she may wish to include family members in
the drawings in place of the regular characters. Use these illustrations
the next time you read the actual book with your child. Older children may
wish to locate illustrations from old children's classics and develop a
brand-new story that can be recorded or written.

Sincerely,

MOTIVATING YOUR CHILD THROUGH TELEVISION

Dear Parents,

Many parents are concerned about the influence of TV on their children's reading development. Television has become a major source of entertainment for many American families and its influence can be felt in several aspects of our daily lives. TV can also have a positive effect on your child's growth in reading. It can spark and illuminate many new and exciting adventures for your child. You may find the following ideas appropriate for blending TV and reading.

1. Note your child's special TV interests and provide him or her with books about those interests.

2. Join your child in watching some of his or her favorite TV programs. Bring up the ideas of cause and effect by asking questions such as: "Why did the character do that?" or "What do you think will happen next?".

3. Listening is a natural TV skill that can be transferred to reading. Select an article about an upcoming TV program or noted TV personality and read it to your child. Ask your child to listen for specific facts or ideas. Give your child opportunities to read TV reviews to you, too.

4. Encourage your child to read the newspaper regularly. Suggest that your child look for articles about TV personalities or special programs.

5. Help your child determine what is real or unreal, fantasy or fact, true or false, on TV. Discuss TV programs your child watches that may involve these elements as well as those which portray different cultures than yours.

READING "SPARKLER" OF THE WEEK: Work with your child to create some puppets similar to those in a favorite book. Use popsicle sticks, cloth, and other materials. Plan a small play to put on for other family members. If possible have a tape recorder to save the "production."

Sincerely,

FAMILY READING ACTIVITIES

Dear Parents,

There are a wide variety of reading activities that all members of the family can participate in together. These kinds of activities can be done while the family is driving somewhere, sitting down at the dinner table, on vacation, or engaged in daily activities. Some of these suggestions should be part of each child's daily "reading lessons." They help to illustrate the fun that can be had with language.

1. Leave lots of notes around the house. These can be positive messages about something your child has done or a reminder about chores or weekend activities. Get in the habit of writing a message instead of saying it.

2. When your child wants to play a familiar game, ask him or her to tell you the directions in the proper order or to write them down. With a new game, ask your child to read the directions to you.

3. Give your child a mail order catalog and ask him or her to locate specific items and read them to you. Or give your child a certain amount of "play money" and ask him or her to locate five items that can be purchased with that amount.

4. When the family is gathered together and talking, ask your child to listen for a particular word (i.e. "money", "school") and write down the number of times it is heard.

5. Put your child in charge of a family calendar. Your child can keep track of dentist appointments, vacation time, school holidays, and upcoming birthdays, etc.

READING "SPARKLER" OF THE WEEK: Have your child make up a colorful poster each month that "advertises" a specific reading topic, such as "sports stories" or "mysteries." Then discuss the books from your home library and list appropriate ones on the poster as possible reading selections for your child. He or she can cut out words from magazine ads as examples ("New", "Exciting", "Be the first on your block...") before or after a book is read.

Sincerely,

SETTING A GOOD EXAMPLE

Dear Parents,

Helping your child develop the skills necessary to become a successful reader can be one of the most important jobs you do. In fact, children's success in reading is often determined by the importance given it by their parents. In other words, parents who value and appreciate reading will tend to have children who also value and appreciate reading.

By setting a good example, you will be helping to show your child that reading can be an important part of his or her life just as it is an important part of your life. Parents who read tend to have children who read as well. You may wish to consider the following points in setting a good example for your child.

1. Set aside a special time each day for all family members to read together. You may wish to use this time as silent reading time or an opportunity for family members to read to each other.

2. Be sure your child has plenty of opportunities to see you reading (and enjoying it). Take some time occasionally to tell your child about some of the things you enjoy reading.

3. Subscribe to magazines and newspapers whenever possible. Children who see lots of reading material coming into the house will be eager to read some of it for themselves.

4. Visit the public library frequently and bring home lots of books. Be sure to check out books for yourself as well as encouraging other family members to do so, too. Keep a constant flow of books coming into the house at all times.

5. Share with your child some interesting topics that you enjoyed as a child. Encourage your child to explore some of the literature you read when you were growing up.

READING "SPARKLER" OF THE WEEK: Make up a map of the location of events in a favorite story of your child. You may wish to look in an atlas or road map. You and your child may even wish to construct an imaginary map and post it in his or her room. Older children may wish to write in a few actual events that took place in special locations and keep these maps beside the corresponding books in the family bookcase.

Sincerely,

PROVIDING ENCOURAGEMENT

Dear Parents,

As children grow up, they naturally look to adults for guidance. Often children develop their own habits and personality based upon what they see parents and other adults do. For example, a child who sees a parent read a great deal will be inclined to want to read, too. Setting a good example involves more than just giving your child lots of books. It also involves a measure of encouragement and respect for your child as he or she grows up. You can contribute greatly to your child's reading development through some of the following practices.

1. Give your child lots of praise as he or she learns new skills in reading. A little praise each day can go a long way toward building successful students.

2. Don't compare your child with others in the family or in the neighborhood. Respect your child as an individual and allow him or her to grow in his or her own special way.

3. Listen to your child and encourage him or her to talk with you. Ask your child to share parts of his or her day with you on a regular basis.

4. Be patient. Remember that growing and learning both take time. Try not to rush your child into something he or she may not be ready to do.

5. Try to have a dictionary, encyclopedia, or some other reference source to check on new words or facts. Be sure to use these regularly yourself.

6. Make books and magazines a regular part of your gift-giving. Birthdays, holidays, or any other occasion provide wonderful opportunities to share the joy of books with your child.

READING "SPARKLER" OF THE WEEK: Obtain a menu from a nearby restaurant. Ask your child to look through old magazines and cut out pictures of food items printed on the menu. Paste these pictures on separate pieces of paper and direct your child to suggest four to five descriptive words for each picture. These words can be printed on each sheet and the sheets collected into a special scrapbook (which can be taken to the restaurant next time you visit). Older children may wish to plan a dinner for the entire family using the menu and a specific amount of money.

Sincerely,

BUILDING POSITIVE ATTITUDES

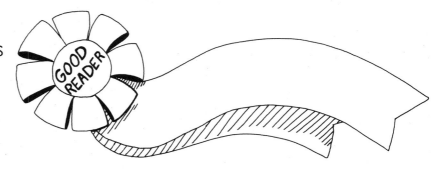

Dear Parents,

Much of a child's personality is determined by the action of others in his or her life. When children see adults sharing ideas and thoughts, children want to share, too. When children experience lots of love and affection in the home, they tend to be affectionate, too. It's not unusual, therefore, for children to imitate adults, especially their parents. The things we do and say often have an effect on the way our children develop, particularly in terms of their self-concept or belief in themselves. Helping children build positive attitudes through good examples can be a most worthwhile parent activity.

A Checklist For Parents: (Check those that are true.)

1. _____ I avoid comparing my child with others.

2. _____ Our family shares lots of care and love.

3. _____ I accept my child as he or she is.

4. _____ I make a special effort to listen to my child.

5. _____ I try new things and encourage my child to do so as well.

6. _____ I try to praise my child regularly.

7. _____ I talk with my child, encouraging him or her to share both happy and sad parts of the day.

8. _____ I read on a regular basis and read to my child regularly, too.

9. _____ I plan time each day when my child and I can play together.

10. _____ I respect my child as a valuable member of the family.

READING "SPARKLER" OF THE WEEK: Get a bag of large dried beans. Take out about fifty and, using a magic marker, print a letter of the alphabet on each one. Put these into a jar and give it to your child. Ask your child to pick out a bean and say a word that begins with that letter. Do this with five or six beans. You may wish to have your child pick out several beans and make up a sentence -- each bean standing for one word in the sentence. Encourage your child to think of some other "letter bean" games, too.

Sincerely,

SELECTING BOOKS WITH YOUR CHILD

Dear Parents,

   Having books to read can be a very important part of the reading development of your child. It teaches your child that reading is a valuable part of his or her life and that books can be a constant source of information and pleasure. Whether you obtain your child's books from the library or the local bookstore, there are several considerations you may wish to keep in mind so that you know you are choosing a book appropriate for your child's age and reading level.

   1. Your child's interests or hobbies can provide the first clue as to the kinds of books he or she will enjoy. The kinds of TV shows your child watches can also give you ideas.

   2. Your child should be allowed some freedom in selecting the books he or she would like to read. If your child chooses easy books, then have your child read to you. If the books are too hard, you can read them to your child.

   3. Encourage your child to pick out books with lots of illustrations. Illustrations can be used as points of discussion between you and your child about story settings and character descriptions. They can add more "life" to a book.

   4. Be sure to discuss with your child the types of books he or she chooses. Make your child feel proud when he or she has made wise choices. This will encourage your child to read more books.

READING "SPARKLER" OF THE WEEK: Obtain a cardboard box and cut out a square in the bottom. Give your child a roll of shelf paper or adding machine tape and ask your child to draw several scenes of a favorite book. Wind the roll on two dowels or toilet tissue rolls placed in both ends of the box. Your child can then show his or her hand-rolled "movie" to other members of the family or friends. Older children may want to write a script for their "movie."

Sincerely,

CHILDREN'S INTERESTS

Dear Parents,

Helping your child discover all the joys of reading will be an important part of your sharing time together. When you take the time to read with your child, you are demonstrating to him or her that reading is an important part of your life. More importantly, however, you can demonstrate that it can also be an important part of your child's life, too.

Making sure your child has sufficient reading material is also a valuable part of this process. Helping your child acquire new books and stories to build his or her personal library is an important parental responsibility.

1. Talk with your child about his or her interests or hobbies. What kinds of things does your child enjoy doing? Help your child select books keyed to those interests.

2. Talk with the school librarian or former teachers and find out the kinds of materials your child has enjoyed in the past. Choose reading materials in line with those interests.

3. Check around your neighborhood or community. Talk with other youngsters the same age as your child (or their parents). Find out what they enjoy reading and choose similar books for your child.

4. If possible, talk with the manager of a local bookstore. Ask him or her to tell you the most popular books that children are reading in your area.

5. Keep an eye on the Sunday paper. Often children's book lists will be published that can provide you with leads for new purchases.

READING "SPARKLER" OF THE WEEK: Check with a local carpet dealer and ask for some free carpet squares. Put these in a corner of your child's room along with some pillows and an old, comfortable chair. Hang some posters and make this a special reading place for your child to go to whenever he or she would like to do some quiet reading. Encourage your child to do some "interior decorating," too.

Sincerely,

SELECTING BOOKS FOR YOUR CHILD: RESOURCES

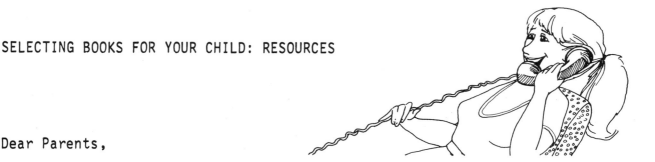

Dear Parents,

You are probably aware of the enormous number of books available for children. There are books of every size, shape, and color. In addition, there are books for a multitude of interests and reading abilities.

You may often ask yourself "How do I find the right book(s) for my child?" While there is no book or books right for every child, there is a wide enough variety that each and every child can enjoy the pleasures of reading for a long time to come.

1. Write to three or four children's book publishers. You can obtain addresses from your local bookstore. Ask each publisher to send you the latest catalog. When it arrives, spend some time with your child selecting possible new purchases.

2. You may want to get a group of parents together to set up a neighborhood cooperative to exchange and share childrens' books among families.

3. Check with a local youth organization (YMCA, Girl's Club) and ask if they have any book related activities during the year. If your child belongs, you can always select books that match the sport or activity in which he or she participates.

4. Have your child interview older members of the family or those in the neighborhood. Encourage your child to ask about the books that were popular when these individuals were youngsters. Would they still be recommended today?

5. Many local public libraries employ children's librarians who will be glad to help you select appropriate books and other reading materials. Don't forget school librarians, too.

READING "SPARKLER" OF THE WEEK: Purchase an inexpensive calendar (or make up one of your own). Select a page from the upcoming month. Ask your child to tell you the names of some of his or her favorite books or stories. Write these randomly in several of the calendar squares. When that date comes up, then the story written in that square is the one you and your child can share together during your story time.

Sincerely,

DEVELOPING GOOD COMPREHENSION

Dear Parents,

   One of the major goals of reading instruction is to help children attain
high levels of comprehension. Children who understand more of what they read
are children who enjoy reading more. Parents can play a vital role in helping
their children attain sound comprehension skills.

   This can occur very naturally during your sharing time together, when
you are reading a story to your child, or even when traveling in the car.
Providing your child with opportunities to reflect and appreciate what he
or she reads can be an important contribution to his or her reading development.

   1. Before you and your child read a story together, ask your child to
       formulate a question about the title or initial illustrations.
       This helps your child develop a reason for reading the story.

   2. Some children enjoy making up their own questions about a story
       after it is read. You may wish to encourage your child to develop
       questions like those on school tests. Take some time to go over
       all the questions.

   3. It is often a good idea to keep a vocabulary notebook or word card
       box nearby when reading stories with your child. This provides an
       opportunity for your child to record any new words, which can be
       defined and written in his or her own sentences.

   4. As you and your child are reading a story together, stop every so
       often and ask your child to draw a picture of a significant event.
       Upon completion of the story, direct your child to arrange these
       pictures in sequential order and/or paste them into a special
       scrapbook.

   5. After you have finished reading a story, ask your child to
       summarize it in as few words as possible. Assist your child in
       coming up with a statement that conveys the main idea of the entire
       story.

READING "SPARKLER" OF THE WEEK: Write your child lots of notes and leave
them in various places around the house (refrigerator, bulletin board). One
unique idea is to write your child a new note each day and pack it in his
or her lunch bag/box. These brief notes are an excellent way to say something
positive to your child.

Sincerely,

COMPREHENSION HINTS

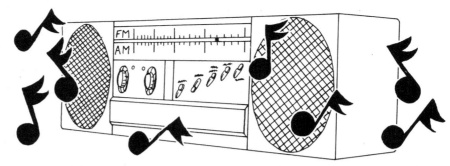

Dear Parents,

One of the most important things children learn in reading is how to comprehend written material. Parents can play a vital role in helping their children understand more of what they do read, not by becoming "teachers" for their children, but rather by encouraging their children to read and think beyond the actual words in a reading selection. The following ideas provide you with some suggestions.

1. Cut out some photos from the newspaper or an old magazine. Ask your child to think of new titles for each picture and write each one on a slip of paper. Encourage your child to combine these into a notebook or scrapbook.

2. As you and your child listen to a popular song, write down some of the lyrics. Afterwards, ask your child to rearrange the lyrics in the correct order. You may want to use such songs as "Jingle Bells" or "Mary Had a Little Lamb" as starters.

3. During a commercial break in a television program you are both watching, ask your child questions such as "Why is the character doing that?" or "What do you think will happen next?". These kind of reasoning/anticipation questions are important in comprehension development.

4. As you read a story to your child, stop every so often and ask your child to think of a word that may come next in the story. Encourage your child to be creative and think of as many words as possible for each "blank."

5. Before you read a familiar story again to your child, ask him or her to give you a capsule summary of the characters, events, or situations that occurred. Encourage your child to keep his or her "review" short and to the point. Compare this summation with the actual events of the story as you read.

READING "SPARKLER" OF THE WEEK: Start up a "reading club" for your child. Provide your child with some special awards or stickers after he or she has read a certain number of books (either independently or with you). These items can be purchased at a variety store or teacher supply store. Better yet, make some up yourself with cardboard and magic markers.

Sincerely,

MORE COMPREHENSION IDEAS

Dear Parents,

     An essential ingredient in good reading is good comprehension. Being
able to say and read words means very little if children are unable to
understand the relationships that exist between words, how sentences and
paragraphs are organized, and how to use this information to further their
own knowledge. Parents can play an important role in assisting their
children in developing sound comprehension skills, not with lots of drills,
but rather with lots of games, love, and encouragement. Try these.

    1. As you read a new story to your child, stop every so often and ask
        your child what he or she thinks will happen next. Help your child
        make predictions about future actions, then read on and see what
        does happen.

    2. Before you read a new book to your child, show him or her the
        illustrations and ask what events he or she thinks will happen in
        the story. Or you may wish to read a picture book to your child
        (without showing the pictures) and ask your child to draw his or
        her own illustrations. Be sure to compare the content of the
        originals with your child's versions rather than artwork.

    3. Talk with your child about some things that have happened during
        the day. Ask your child to draw separate illustrations of each
        event on a sheet of paper and to arrange them in the correct
        chronological order.

    4. Ask your child to dictate or write a summary of a favorite
        children's song. How could the song be summarized in twenty-five
        words or less? In ten words or less?

    5. As you read a familiar story to your child, make four or five
        intentional errors (name of character, setting, action). Ask
        your child to listen carefully and identify each mistake.

READING "SPARKLER" OF THE WEEK: Ask your child to dictate a sentence to you.
Print each word of the sentence on a separate index card. Mix up the cards
and give them to your child to put in the correct order. Then have your
child use the sentence in a "made-up" story. Do this with other sentences,
too. Encourage older children to share longer sentences.

Sincerely,

THE IMPORTANCE OF QUESTIONS

Dear Parents,

Questions help your child focus on the important elements of reading and their probable causes or effects. There are many opportunities during the day when you and your child can share questions. But question-asking should not be limited to only reading time. It can be a normal and natural part of each family's daily activities. Most importantly, it can become an important part of your child's reading development.

1. Ask your child lots of questions that begin with the word "Why." These questions encourage active thinking and help your child explore the reasons for certain events or occurances, both in books and everyday life. For example: "Why do we need traffic signals?", "Why do some animals live underground?", or "Why do we have to wear shoes?".

2. Provide your child with opportunities to ask questions, too. For example, when you and your youngster select a book to read, ask your child to pose one or two questions about the title on the cover of the book. Before your child begins reading the book, encourage him or her to develop additional questions about the story that can be written on a sheet of paper. After completing the story, take some time to talk over and discuss the questions your child posed.

3. Some of the most important kinds of questions you can share are those that relate to your child's personal experiences. For example, how would a certain story have been different if your child were the main character? What things did the characters in a favorite book do that your child has done? Has your child seen or visited places similar to those that were mentioned in a recently read story?

READING "SPARKLER" OF THE WEEK: Collect several copies of old children's books at a yard or garage sale. Remove several of the pages from the middle of a book. Ask your child to read the book and suggest some possible actions for the missing part. Your child may wish to compare his or her contributions with the actual story content.

Sincerely,

STORY QUESTIONS

Dear Parents,

Questions help children discover more about the world in which they live -- whether that world is their living room, a community park, or a large city. Questions help children acquire new knowledge and gain an appreciation of the "how and why" of life. Parents, too, can participate in asking their children questions, not to test how much their offsprings know, but rather to help their children focus on important points of discovery. Try these.

1. What do you think this story will be about?

2. Do you know about any other books on this topic? Tell me about them.

3. Where do you think this story might take place?

4. Has the author of this book written any other books that you have read? Tell me about them.

5. How do you think this story will turn out?

6. Did the story turn out as you expected?

7. What made this an interesting or uninteresting story?

8. What might be some new things we could add to the ending?

9. Is the main character someone you would like to have as a friend? Why or why not?

10. Is this a book your friends would enjoy reading? Why or why not?

READING "SPARKLER" OF THE WEEK: Punch a small hole in the top and bottom of several uncooked eggs and blow out the contents. Help your child draw the faces of some characters in a favorite book on each egg with crayons or markers. Your child can then put these "puppets" over a pencil and act out a portion of the story for other family members. Encourage your child to set up a display in his or her room of these characters.

Sincerely,

ASKING EVERYDAY QUESTIONS

Dear Parents,

There are many ways that you can assist your child in becoming the best reader possible. Some of these methods do not even involve books or stories, rather they involve thinking strategies -- thinking strategies that lead to reading discoveries. It is important to remember that reading is actually a thinking process, one in which we gather new or interesting information and make it a part of our lives. By helping your child think more about the world in which he or she lives, you will be assisting in the development of strategies that foster reading development. Children who are encouraged to think and question their environment are children who develop good comprehension skills. You can stimulate your child's thinking powers by asking questions for which there may be many possible answers. You and your child may want to use some of the following as examples.

1. Why do we have lines painted on the street?

2. Where does the wind go?

3. How tall can trees grow?

4. Why do we have to wear clothes?

5. What do some animals do when it gets dark?

6. Why do animals need to drink water?

7. Why are there so many different colors?

READING "SPARKLER" OF THE WEEK: Provide your child with a few simple props (chair, box, brush, pencil, etc.) and ask him or her to pantomime a favorite story or book. Ask other family members to guess the name of the book. Other family members may wish to take turns pantomiming their favorite children's books, too.

Sincerely,

VOCABULARY GROWTH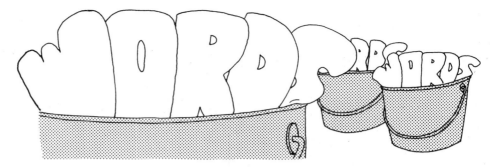

Dear Parents,

Development of a large vocabulary is an important part of your child's growth in reading. Children learn new words by having opportunities to use them many times in talking, reading, and writing. Providing your child with many exposures to words helps him or her gain an appreciation for how words are used in our language and builds a solid foundation for later reading success. It's not necessary for children to memorize long lists of words, but it is important for them to use words in many different situations. Here are some examples.

1. Each family member can attempt to learn a new word each day. All the family members will benefit.

2. As you talk to your child, use new words frequently. Put them in sentences that he or she can understand. For example, "That was an enormous elephant. Look how big it is."

3. Remember that children need many repetitions of words before those words become a natural part of their vocabularies. Try to share new words with your child in a variety of situations.

4. Read lots of books to your child. The more opportunities children have to hear words in action, the more inclined they will be to add those words to their own vocabularies.

READING "SPARKLER" OF THE WEEK: Share some crossword puzzles with your child. Inexpensive ones can be obtained at any book store. Work with your child in creating your own puzzles using some of your child's favorite words.

Sincerely,

LEARNING NEW WORDS

Dear Parents,

Learning about words and their meanings will be a very valuable part of our discoveries in reading this year. It is also a very important part of your child's success in reading and all his or her other subjects, too. Parents can play a very important role in assisting their children to acquire a large storehouse of words as well as providing them with many opportunities to use those words as they talk, write, or read. Vocabulary development, however, doesn't mean memorizing long lists of words or looking up lots of words in the dictionary. More importantly, it means using words in a variety of learning situations. Here are some suggestions.

1. Occasionally, ask your child to listen for any new words that he or she doesn't know and would like to learn. Print these on separate index cards, decorate them if you wish, and present them to your child. Help your child keep these in a special box or carton. Using them in sentences with a clear meaning will also be helpful.

2. Work with your child to label various items around your house. Direct your child to point to objects in the house (chair, bed, coffee pot) and name them. Print the word for each item on a piece of paper and tape it to the item. Give your child several opportunities to read these words over the next several days.

3. Cut out unknown words from newspaper headlines. You may wish to have your child use each word in his or her own sentence.

4. Read a paragraph or two of one of your favorite books. Talk with your child about the ways some of the words are used. Be sure to share your enthusiasm for the many uses of certain words.

READING "SPARKLER" OF THE WEEK: If your child has a pet or stuffed animal, let him or her read to it occasionally. This "silent audience" gives your child an opportunity to share the joy of reading with a non-critical audience and in a non-threatening way. Adding an easy-to-use tape recorder once in a while will allow you to listen later. Older children should be encouraged to read to younger brothers or sisters.

Sincerely,

A STRONG VOCABULARY

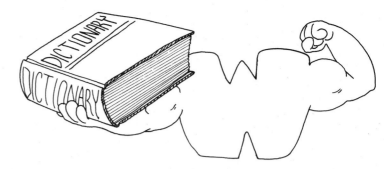

Dear Parents,

Learning about new words can be an exciting part of reading development. Words are the vehicles we use to take us into new stories and adventures. They help us understand AND learn more about the world around us. Words are important for your child, too. Your child's growth in vocabulary will be an important part of our work in reading this year. A strong vocabulary will help your child in many subjects besides reading. You can help your child develop and appreciate new words. Sharing words and their meanings in a relaxed, natural atmosphere can be an important part of your time together.

1. Encourage your child to share new words with you. What new words has he or she found today in his or her books and magazines or what new words were heard on TV or radio? Encourage your child to be alert for new words and their uses.

2. Share with your child the words you have discovered. If your child sees that you enjoy words and their uses, he or she will appreciate them, too.

3. Encourage your child to read from a variety of printed materials. The more words your child encounters in reading, the more valuable they will become for him or her.

4. Help your child understand that many words have multiple meanings. Demonstrate how other words in a sentence help define a new word.

READING "SPARKLER" OF THE WEEK: Take a walk with your child around your neighborhood. Try to locate five new words (on buildings, the street, signs, etc.) and write them down. Talk with your child about how each word is used, its meaning, and the importance of its location. Upon your return home, ask your child to make a simple map indicating where each word was found. Older children might like to learn new concepts such as a "chain link fence" or "swag curtains."

Sincerely,

READING AND WRITING

Dear Parents,

     Writing can be an important part of your child's development in
reading. Writing activities help strengthen reading skills as well as
provide an additional opportunity for your child to communicate with others.
Encouraging your child to write ideas, sentences, or stories on a regular
basis will help him or her appreciate the value of printed words.   The
following are some ideas you should consider to help your child become a
regular writer AND reader.

    1.   Encourage your child to talk about ideas and jot down these ideas
         before a writing activity begins. Be sure to give your child lots
         of praise as she or he begins to write.

    2.   Provide a corner for your child to write. Paper, pencil, and
         erasers should be placed on your child's desk or table. Your
         child should have a private place for writing AND homework.

    3.   It is important for you and your child to set time for writing
         together. Be patient and encouraging when your child can't think
         of anything to write. If necessary, ask your child to begin
         telling you a story for you to write down.

    4.   Let your child see you write notes, lists, letters, and stories.
         It is a good idea for your child to see you make revisions.
         Children should see that writing takes place at home just as it
         does at school.

    5.   Writing skills develop slowly and at different rates for different
         children. Encourage your child to share ideas. Don't worry about
         mistakes in grammar, spelling, or punctuation until your child has
         finished writing and is ready to jazz up the ideas.

READING "SPARKLER" OF THE WEEK: Ask your child to write a letter to the author
of a favorite book. If necessary, you may wish to have your child dictate
the letter to you which can then be typed. Send this letter in care of this
author's publisher. You and your child may discover a reply in the mail a
few weeks later. Be sure to have your child bring the reply to school to
share.

Sincerely,

Dear Parents,

Reading and writing naturally go together. Each helps to reinforce the other and establish the importance of good communication for your child. By helping your child practice writing skills, you are also helping your child develop sound reading skills. Children of any age can become involved in writing activities. The possibilities are endless. By making writing a fun and exciting part of your sharing time, you will be helping to ensure that your child gains a valuable communication skill. The following are some ideas to do together.

1. Encourage your child to write a brief description of a TV program you have recently seen. Ask your child to compare his or her description to the one in the TV schedule.

2. Work with your child to put together a list of new words heard during the week. These could be words heard in school, on television, or at meals. Ask your child to create sentences using some of these words.

3. Encourage your child to create a monthly family newspaper. Using the daily paper for format, help your child to interview family members and write up fashion, sports, front page, comics, or other "newsworthy" sections. Pictures from the family album can be used for added effect.

4. Cut out several pictures from old magazines and paste them on sheets of paper. Ask your child to create captions for each one and write the titles under each photo.

5. Your child may wish to keep a diary of personal or family events. Provide your child with the option of sharing or not sharing these with other family members. Honor his or her decision.

READING "SPARKLER" OF THE WEEK: After you and your child have read a story together, ask your child to make up a list of words in the story that describe a) taste, b) smell, c) hearing, d) touch, or e) sight. Encourage your child to add new words to the lists as other stories are read. Your child may wish to locate items in the house that words on his or her list describe.

Sincerely,

PROVIDING MANY EXPERIENCES

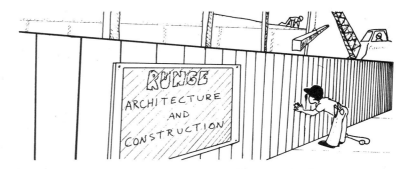

Dear Parents,

　　One of the most valuable things you can do for your child to help him
or her succeed in reading is to offer many experiences outside the home.
Children who have had opportunities to see and explore the wide world
outside are children who understand more of what they read.

　　For instance, a child who has seen a building under construction will
have a much better concept of buildings when they are encountered in stories
and books. A child who has been to a planetarium or gone fishing, for
example, has a strong foundation of experiences to contribute to future
reading on these subjects. Reading comprehension is built upon the experiences
children bring to the printed page. Here are some suggestions.

　　1.　As you work around the house, share your job with your child. Take
　　　　some time to talk about the various parts of the work you are doing
　　　　(fixing a faucet, sewing on a button) and, if practical, let your
　　　　child participate in the activity, too.

　　2.　Take your child on "field trips" around the house. Look in the
　　　　basement, attic, or different rooms and talk with your child about
　　　　the sights and sounds you discover. You may even find new
　　　　"treasures" in old familiar rooms.

　　3.　Plan a "trip" around your neighborhood with your child. Take a
　　　　walk and talk about some of the things you see and hear. Your
　　　　child may wish to prepare a mini-scrapbook to record some of the
　　　　things discovered on these trips.

　　4.　Plan a car trip to someplace away from your town or city. Help
　　　　your child look at a road map and discuss some of the sights you
　　　　may see. If possible, bring a camera and take pictures of newly
　　　　discovered items.

　　5.　Every once in a while, take your child to the public library and
　　　　look through magazines about distant places. Talk about some of
　　　　the unusual sights you discover and any similarities or differences
　　　　found.

READING "SPARKLER" OF THE WEEK: Write, or have your child write, the names
of his or her favorite stories on separate pieces of paper. Put them in a
bag or box. Each day, have your child select one title. This is the story
you will read to him or her that day.

Sincerely,

LEARNING FROM EXPERIENCES

Dear Parents,

        Childhood is filled with many new and exciting experiences. Helping
your child discover and appreciate these experiences will be an important
part of his or her growth in reading -- both now and for the future.
Readers tend to use the experiences they have encountered in their lives as
a foundation for understanding and enjoying the ideas in books and magazines.
Helping your child succeed in reading can be stimulated by offering a variety
of experiences outside the home, in the community, the neighborhood, and
beyond. Try these ideas.

    1. Plan a simple family project such as planting a small garden,
        building a simple bookcase, or preparing for a party. Be sure to
        involve your child in the various stages and talk about the steps
        involved. Your child may wish to record some of these in a small
        notebook.

    2. Take time to visit some community buildings. The post office,
        fire or police station, or city hall all offer wonderful
        opportunities for your child to expand his or her world of
        experiences.

    3. Many industries conduct tours of their plants or factories. Call
        them and ask if you can arrange a tour for the family. Be sure to
        bring a camera and encourage your child to ask lots of questions.

    4. Visit the airport, shopping mall, or downtown section of a nearby
        town where lots of people come and go. Discuss with your child
        the different people that you see. Ask your child to guess what
        they may be doing or what their jobs may be.

    5. Help your child develop a new hobby or interest (building models,
        photography, collecting stamps). Show your child all the
        information available on that hobby in books and magazines. You
        may wish to locate and visit other hobbyists who can share some
        new information with your child.

READING "SPARKLER" OF THE WEEK: Take an old photograph or magazine picture
and glue it to stiff cardboard. Cut it into several jigsaw pieces and mix
them up. Direct your child to reassemble the picture and make up a story
about it. The puzzle can then be placed in an envelope or kept in a box. As
you add more puzzles, identify all the pieces to the same puzzle by writing
the same number on each piece and labeling the envelope with that number and
an appropriate title.

Sincerely,

EXPERIENCES LEAD TO READING

Dear Parents,

The experiences we have during our childhood are often the ones we remember most vividly. Children encounter many new experiences every day, each one having some small impact on that child's growth and development. Whether it be the discovery of an autumn leaf or seeing a newborn kitten for the first time, a child's world is ripe for many discoveries. It is these experiences that form the foundation for later reading comprehension and understanding.

In other words, reading becomes more personal for a child when he or she can base it on actual experiences. Parents can play a vital role in helping their children discover many new experiences.

1. Work with your child to create a notebook about faraway places. Cut out photos from old magazines or newspapers. Paste these on sheets of paper and write some captions for them.

2. If you have a camera or can borrow one, visit a new area in your community and take some pictures. Discuss some of the things in each one after the prints have been received.

3. Plan a special trip to the zoo, museum, opera house, arboretum, game preserve, aquarium, or farm. Encourage your child to help plan the trip and be sure to take time to talk about it afterwards.

4. Pull out old family albums or documents. Talk with your child about the family history, some of your child's ancestors, and where family members have lived. Your child may want to put together a special scrapbook of recent family history.

5. Read books to your child about the past. Discuss with him or her the similarities or differences in the way we live now.

READING "SPARKLER" OF THE WEEK: Work with your child to create a small indoor garden. Put some soil in small milk cartons and plant several varieties of flower or vegetable seeds. Share the directions on the seed packets with your child concerning planting depth, watering instructions, and length of time until maturity. Help your child keep a notebook about this mini-garden.

Sincerely,

USING CHILDREN'S MAGAZINES

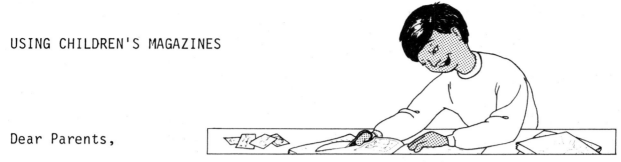

Dear Parents,

    One of the best ways you can help stimulate the reading habit in your child is by subscribing to a children's magazine. Any child who has ever gotten his or her own mail knows the joy that comes from reading and listening to something created just for him or her. Children's magazines contain a wealth of valuable activities and projects that can stimulate reading and encourage the development of creative thinking. A child who regularly receives a magazine will undoubtedly be a child who wants to read on his or her own. The following are some ideas for using children's magazines.

    1. After your child has collected several magazines, ask him or her to select some favorite stories, remove them from the magazine, paste each to a sheet of construction paper, and sew them together with yarn. These collections can then be added to your child's library.

    2. Remove one or two stories from several magazines and cut off the endings (the last two to three paragraphs). Read each story to your child and ask him or her to suggest appropriate endings. Match each of your child's endings with the originals.

    3. Cut out a story from a magazine and remove any pictures. After you and your child have shared the story together, ask him or her to draw some new and original illustrations. They can be compared (in content, not artwork) to the original illustrations later.

    4. Be sure to play the games and work on the projects in the magazines together with your child. By sharing these activities you will be helping your child appreciate your interest in his or her learning.

    5. Occasionally, you and your child will discover advertisements for various catalogs in children's magazines. Send for these (using your child's name) and when they arrive share them with your child. Help your child understand that reading includes more than just books and magazines.

READING "SPARKLER" OF THE WEEK: Help your child locate clothing or objects that a character in a favorite book may have worn. Your child may wish to dress up as a character and reinact a portion of the story. You may also wish to set up a special display in the house with a copy of the book, some clothing, an illustration or two, and/or some objects located in the house.

Sincerely,

CHILDREN'S BOOK CLUBS

Dear Parents,

One of the greatest gifts you can give your child is the gift of reading. Children who grow up in a reading environment are children who appreciate all the joys and wonders in books. One way you can help develop the reading habit for your child is by having him or her join a children's book club. Imagine the look on your child's face every month or so as he or she receives a package addressed specifically to him or her! The excitement of opening his or her own package and discovering a new adventure, thrilling mystery, fascinating biography, or imaginative story is surely a stimulus to reading enjoyment for your child. The time and effort can certainly be a positive dimension of your child's growth in reading. The following guidelines can help you select an appropriate club.

1. Will the binding of the books last a long time?

2. Are the illustrations of high quality? Are there too many or too few?

3. Is the size of print too small or too large?

4. Are the stories the right length for your child?

5. Is there a large variety in the type of literature such as poems, games, stories, etc.?

6. How many books will you need to purchase in the next year?

7. Are you allowed to cancel the membership at any time? Is there a minimum number of purchases?

8. Are you permitted free inspection of the books before buying?

9. Are there sufficient selections that match the interests of your child?

READING "SPARKLER" OF THE WEEK: Cut out pictures from old magazines of unusual objects or animals which are not found in your part of the country. Paste these on sheets of paper. Every so often, ask your child to make up a story about the object or animal or to suggest descriptive words that may tell about it. Encourage your child to use his or her imagination. These stories or words can be written on the sheet for display in his or her room.

Sincerely,

IN THE PUBLIC LIBRARY

Dear Parents,

    The public library can be an important part of your child's education.
Not only does it contain thousands of books, but it can also offer your child
a variety of reading-related activities, both during the school year as well
as during vacation times. Encouraging your child to make the library a
regular part of his or her reading experiences can be a positive way of
stimulating a lifelong reading habit. The following are some activities and
programs that the public library may offer you and your child.

    1. Make sure your family has a family library card. Some libraries
        will permit students to sign up for their own cards.

    2. Some libraries have special story hours for youngsters of all ages,
        as well as "Meet the Authors" and discussion groups. Check with
        your local librarians for the times and days in your town.

    3. Often the library will schedule special workshops for children.
        These sessions will provide opportunities for young readers to
        create book-related projects such as mobiles, dioramas, and posters.

    4. Many libraries have a Reference Librarian who can be of invaluable
        assistance in locating homework information. Many times this
        information can be obtained with just a simple phone call.

    5. Many libraries have sections especially for parents. Included may
        be books on parenting, special workshops or classes, or family
        booklists available for the asking.

READING "SPARKLER" OF THE WEEK: Ask your child to illustrate the most exciting
(or saddest, scariest) part of a recently read book. These pictures may be
appropriate for display in your child's room, the family room or even on the
referigerator door.

Sincerely,

PUBLIC LIBRARY SERVICES

Dear Parents,

Your local public library can provide your child with rich and valuable experiences with books and reading. Many libraries realize that children who develop the reading habit early will become lifelong readers. For that reason, many libraries offer a variety of services designed to appeal to both children and families alike. Investigate your local library with your child and discover the many things that are in store for you.

1. Many community libraries have bookmobiles that make regular trips into several neighborhoods. Try to find out when and where the bookmobile will be in your area and be sure to take your child for a visit.

2. Some libraries stock collections of children's games and puzzles. Most of these are educational in nature and can help in the development of reading-related skills.

3. Don't forget the library during vacation times. Many libraries offer special programs during the summer or other holiday times. Call and check on what's happening at your library.

4. Check with your local library to see if they offer a special series of children's films. These films, often keyed to popular children's books, can be a powerful stimulus in helping your child expand his or her reading horizons.

5. When you go out shopping, make your local library a part of the trip. Stop by and pick up a new book for your child as a regular part of your "shopping list."

READING "SPARKLER" OF THE WEEK: Write your child's name in large letters vertically on a large piece of paper. As you and your child share new books, look for characters whose names begin with the letters in your child's name. Record the character names opposite the letters in your child's name on the paper until all letters are completed. Encourage your child to decorate and illustrate the sheet.

Sincerely,

USING THE NEWSPAPER

Dear Parents,

Newspapers are a source of reading material available to many homes. They are inexpensive, readily available, and can be an important part of your child's reading growth. Newspapers offer topics that are current and relevant in addition to offering your child hundreds of activities and ideas that stimulate reading development. You may find some of the following ideas appropriate for you and your child to share together.

1. Ask your child to cut out four to five headlines from the newspaper. Give them to your child and direct him or her to create new stories for each headline. Your child may wish to tell these stories to you or write them in a notebook.

2. Ask your child to make up positive headlines that include the names of family members. Your child may wish to post these for all to see.

3. Ask your child to cut out letters from newspaper headlines to create his or her own words. These words can be pasted on cardboard or index cards to save. Sentences can also be made.

4. Direct your child to look at furniture ads and cut out those items that belong in the bedroom, kitchen, living room, den, etc. These can be pasted on different sheets of paper. Do the same activity for food groups, kinds of clothing, models of cars, etc.

5. Check to see if a local or nearby newspaper has a Newspaper In Education (NIE) program. If so, ask them for a free guide to their materials.

READING "SPARKLER" OF THE WEEK: Work with your child to create an advertisement for a recently read book. Look at several examples in old magazines or newspapers and have your child create an original one for a favorite story. Your child may wish to "sell" his or her book to other family members.

Sincerely,

NEWSPAPER ACTIVITIES

Dear Parents,

The daily newspaper contains a wealth of learning activities that can be used to help your child in reading. It is probably the world's most inexpensive textbook and, best of all, it can come to your front door every day. Familiarizing your child with the sections, activities, and projects in your paper can lead to greater reading competence. The daily newspaper can be an important way for your child to have a constant yet everchanging source of reading material in the house. You and your child can discover dozens of ways to use the newspaper as a source of reading games and activities. Here are some starters.

1. Cut out several words from newspaper headlines and ask your child to put them in alphabetical order.

2. Cut out several pictures from the newspaper and the accompanying captions. Separate the captions from the pictures, mix them up, and direct your child to match each photo with the correct caption.

3. Pick out an ad from the sports page or fashion section and ask your child to point to all the words he or she knows. Print these on a separate piece of paper and paste the ad to this paper.

4. Cut out a comic strip and ask your child to make up four to five questions about it that can be shared with other family members.

5. Point to selected words in headlines and ask your child to think of a rhyming word for each one. Keep lists of these words.

READING "SPARKLER" OF THE WEEK: Cut out letters from the newspaper and tape them on the black squares of a checkerboard. Play a game of checkers with your child, but before anyone can "land" on a square, the player must say one word that begins with that letter. Later, you may wish to make the game more challenging by stating that every word used must be different or that two words must be named for each letter. You may also want to put words on each square with each player required to use a word in a sentence before landing on that space.

Sincerely,

NEWSPAPER FUN

Dear Parents,

The daily newspaper offers many learning opportunities for your child.
It can be used to supplement the books and stories your child reads or
listens to you read. Newspapers are a rich source of games and other
activities that remain fresh and interesting throughout the year.

It makes no difference what grade your child is in -- there is a wealth
of reading opportunities in a newspaper. With a little imagination, you and
your child may discover dozens of projects and activities that can make
learning to read an exciting part of your sharing time together. As a parent,
you can help your child feel comfortable with the newspaper. Try these
activities.

1. Cut out a picture or ad from the paper. Show it to your child and
    say "I see something that begins with the letter 't'." Ask your
    child to point out the object. Do this with other pictures and
    other letters.

2. Cut out a section of an article and ask your child to put a circle
    around all the vowels, or all the consonants, or all the two-
    syllable words.

3. Select certain words from advertisements or the weather report
    and ask your child to suggest antonyms (words opposite in meaning).

4. Cut out a comic strip from the paper and remove the last block. Share
    the strip with your child and ask him or her to suggest a possible
    ending for the strip. Compare his or her ending with the actual one.

5. On separate index cards, write several descriptive words (i.e. large,
    tiny, beautiful). Ask your child to choose several cards and locate
    photos in the paper that can be described with one of the words.

READING "SPARKLER" OF THE WEEK: Get several clothespins and on each one
write a descriptive word such as blue, large, plaid, or sharp. Ask your child
to go through the house and clip each clothespin to an object that can be
described with the appropriate word. Later ask your child to put the clothespins on other objects that can also be described in the same way. "Write up"
new clothespins every so often.

Sincerely,

INFORMATION AGENCIES

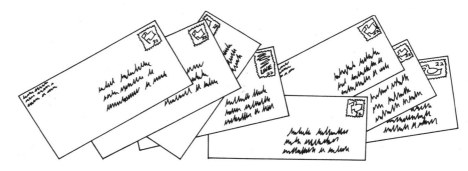

Dear Parents,

Helping your child in reading can be a most exciting part of your child's growth and development. While it is extremely important that this time together be relaxed and unhurried, you may also discover the need for more ideas and information than these letters can provide. Fortunately, there are many organizations which can provide you with a variety of suggestions and information useful in helping your child succeed in reading as well as other aspects of life. You may wish to contact some of these agencies in order to obtain additional ideas.

1. Send a self-addressed, stamped envelope to obtain a folder entitled "Choosing a Child's Book" which describes several lists of books for children. Write to: Children's Book Council, 67 Irving Place, New York, N.Y. 10003.

2. To obtain a list of over 200 recommended books for all ages, send fifteen cents to: Superintendent of Documents, U.S. Government Printing Office, Washington, D.C. 20402.

3. The Consumer Information Center has a catalog of many free or inexpensive items appropriate for parents. One item is "A Family Guide to Television." To obtain a catalog of other items, write to: Consumer Information Center, Pueblo, CO 81009.

4. One organization that can provide you with a wealth of information is the National P.T.A. Write to: National P.T.A., 700 N. Rush St., Chicago, IL 60611.

READING "SPARKLER" OF THE WEEK: If possible, obtain some old photographs or slides from relatives or grandparents. Ask your child to create a special story for selected ones which can be recorded or written.

Sincerely,

SPECIAL PARENT BROCHURES

Dear Parents,

Many organizations and groups provide materials and services that can
be helpful in working with your child. Much of the information these groups
provide is free or available for a very small fee. Kinds of information
available may include: tips on working with your child, the importance of
good nutrition, inexpensive games to make, and recommended lists of books.
Private as well as public organizations can send you a wealth of material
that will not only help your child in reading, but in all your child's school
subjects.

One organization that is very concerned about the role of parents in
their children's reading development is the International Reading Association.
They have a number of parent brochures you may wish to obtain. Single copies
of the following eight brochures are available free by sending a #10 self-
addressed, stamped envelope (with first class postage for two ounces) to:
IRA, 800 Barksdale Rd., P.O. Box 8139, Newark, DE 19714-8139.

1. <u>Your Home is Your Child's First School</u>

2. <u>You Can Encourage Your Child to Read</u>

3. <u>Good Books Make Reading Fun for Your Child</u>

4. <u>Summer Reading is Important</u>

5. <u>You Can Use Television to Simulate Your Child's Reading Habits</u>

6. <u>Studying: A Key to Success...Ways Parents Can Help</u>

7. <u>You Can Help Your Child in Reading by Using the Newspaper</u>

8. <u>Eating Well Can Help Your Child Learn Better</u>

READING "SPARKLER" OF THE WEEK: Cut out shapes of fish from stiff cardboard
and attach a paper clip to each one. Ask your child for some favorite words
and print one on each "fish." Tie a magnet to a stick and place the fish
in a bowl. Direct your child to fish for a word. For each fish "caught,"
ask your child to make up two different sentences using that word.

Sincerely,

FREE BOOK LISTS

Dear Parents,

        It is not unusual for parents to be amazed at the number of children's books available on the market. While many parents want to provide their children with new books on a regular basis, trying to locate the "right" ones is often difficult. A single trip into the local bookstore will reveal a tremendous number of books for all ages, abilities, and interests. Fortunately, there are several groups who can help you select and choose books that are appropriate for your child. Some of them are mentioned below.

    1. Send a stamped, self-addressed envelope to: The Association for Library Service to Children, 50 East Huron St., Chicago, IL 60611 and ask for their annual publication of Caldecott Medal Books and Newberry Medal Books.

    2. For an annotated list of books rated by children as the best each year, send a stamped, self-addressed envelope (with postage for two ounces) to: International Reading Association, 800 Barksdale Road, P.O. Box 8139, Newark, DE 19714-8139. Ask for a current copy of "Children's Choices."

    3. A guide to books appropriate for all ages of children is "Choosing Books for Children: A Commonsense Guide." It can be ordered by sending $2.95 plus $1.25 postage and handling to: Dell Publishing Co., 1 Dag Hammarskjold Plaza, 245 East 47th St., New York, N.Y. 10017.

    4. "Notable Children's Books" is an annual guide listing the best books of the year. It can be obtained by sending a stamped, self-addressed envelope to: The Association for Library Service to Children, 50 East Huron St., Chicago, IL 60611.

READING "SPARKLER" OF THE WEEK: Obtain a large sheet of newsprint or poster paper (available from a stationary or art supply store) and help your child make a poster of his or her four favorite books. You may wish to include illustrations of favorite characters, a book jacket cover or two, new words discovered in the stories, related pictures cut out of old magazines, or even photos of your child reading the book(s). Be sure to put the poster in a prominent place for all to see.

Sincerely,

WINTER VACATION ACTIVITIES

Dear Parents,

Vacation time during the winter months usually centers around various holiday activities. Families are often busy with many different activities -- visiting friends, shopping and exchanging gifts, and attending celebrations. Even though this is a very busy time of the year, it is also important for parents and children to plan some time to relax and share thoughts and books with each other. Make the holiday time a family reading time, too. Help your child understand that reading is not only related to school activities, but is also a vital part of all family activities. Here are some ideas.

1. Take some time each day to have family discussions. Talk about favorite books read, memorable stories, or just "made-up" stories to share with each other. Holiday stories can be included.

2. Help your child make up a scrapbook of words that go with the holiday season. Ask your child to draw illustrations or use the words in different sentences.

3. Locate copies of songs or poems that relate to this time of year. Share these with your child and discuss what some of the words or ideas mean.

4. If you are preparing any special meals, give your child an opportunity to help you. He or she can read recipes to you or help in meal preparation.

5. With your child as a major character, encourage him or her to make up a special holiday story. Write or type the story for your child and share it with neighbors or friends.

READING "SPARKLER" OF THE WEEK: Make up special bingo cards by dividing a piece of paper into twenty-five squares. Print twenty-five words, one to a square on the paper and the same words each on separate index cards. Direct your child to turn over each card and match it with a word on the sheet. Buttons or beans can be used as markers. Tell your child to yell "Bingo" when five words in a row are matched. You and your child may wish to make up other bingo games using other lists of words, too.

Sincerely,

SPRING VACATION ACTIVITIES

Dear Parents,

    Watching children grow and develop can be one of the most exciting parts of parenthood. Helping your child explore and learn more about himself or herself as well as about the world provides families with many sharing opportunities together. With the spring vacation time approaching, you and your child can take advantage of many new opportunities to work and learn together. Best of all, these times together can also be a valuable part of your child's reading development. Here are some suggestions.

1. Be sure to keep reading to your child. While vacations may be a short time away from school, it doesn't mean that reading should be forgotten. Keep the reading habit active.

2. If the weather permits, take a walk outside with your child. Try to discover any new plants or animals around your house or in your neighborhood. Get some books and read more about them.

3. Keep up the library habit, too. Make sure the public library is on your list of family activities this vacation time.

4. Why not encourage your child to develop a new hobby or interest? What materials would you need? Where could you go to discover more information? A visit to a hobby or toy store may be your first stop.

5. Are there yard sales, garage sales, or community sales in your neighborhood? If so, take your child and look for some children's books. Often these can be obtained at a fraction of their original cost and can provide many hours of happy new discoveries for your child.

READING "SPARKLER" OF THE WEEK: Cut the top off of two pint size milk cartons. Force one carton inside the other. On squares of paper, write down six of your child's new or favorite words and paste each square on a side of this "die." Roll the die and ask your child to use the word that comes up in a sentence or story. Other cubes can be made with the names of favorite stories printed on them. When a story title comes up, ask your child to summarize the story for you.

Sincerely,

SUMMER VACATION ACTIVITIES

Dear Parents,

Summer vacation is almost here and along with it come many opportunities for you and your child to share new discoveries in reading. While many children may see summer as a chance to be away from school, it is also a good time to help your child understand the value of reading in everything we do. There are a variety of summertime activities that you and your child can share together that will help reinforce the skills learned in the classroom as well as stimulate many positive experiences with reading. Here are some suggestions.

1. Keep reading with your child. Let your child know that summertime also means reading time, too.

2. Take trips to the library. Many libraries have special summer programs designed just for kids.

3. Provide your child with some quiet reading time. Set aside fifteen or twenty minutes each day for your child to relax and curl up with a good book.

4. For those occasional rainy days, have some reading games on hand. Games such as Scrabble, Spill and Spell, Boggle, and Sentence Cubes all emphasize reading skills.

5. When planning a trip, involve your child as much as possible. Encourage your child to read about the places to be visited, map out possible routes, or design a special scrapbook to record events.

READING "SPARKLER" OF THE WEEK: Obtain some pieces of colored construction paper and trace outlines of rocket ships, stars, or your child's favorite design on each. Cut these out and store in the family bookcase. Whenever your child completes a book this summer, print the title on one of these designs and post on the refrigerator (or other appropriate spot). Offer your child special awards when five, ten, or some other designated number of books have been completed.

Sincerely,

Special
Energizers

SPECIAL ENERGIZERS

The following eighteen ''SPECIAL ENERGIZERS'' are designed to provide parents with more in-depth information on topics contained within the parent letters. They will provide you, the teacher, with a variety of ideas to offer to parents to help promote reading in the home.

There are several ways these pages can be used. First, the materials can be sent home to individual parents who request particular information in response to one of the periodic evaluation letters you are encouraged to use. Second, the SPECIAL ENERGIZERS can be sent home attached to the parent letters which address the same topic. Third, they may be useful to distribute during parent-teacher conferences if the conferences are scheduled at convenient times. Finally, these support materials may be used as a basis for several workshops for parents.

Included for your convenience is the following list which matches each of the SPECIAL ENERGIZERS with the parent letter(s) that deal(s) with the same topic.

Special Energizers	Parent Letters
A. Family Reading Check-up	#7, #8, #9
B. Book Sharing Questions	#14, #15, #16
C. Interest Inventory	#12
D. Lots of Things to Read	#5, #25
E. Words of Encouragement	#9, #10
F. Magazines for Children	#28
G. Listening Checklist	#17, #18, #19
H. Reading with Your Child: Five Easy Steps	#3, #4
I. Using Games	#20, #21, #22
J. Travel Games	#40
K. Comprehension Tips	#14, #15, #16
L. Suggestions for Improving Comprehension	#14, #15, #16
M. Resources for Parents	#35, #36, #37
N. Tuning in to Reading and Television	#6
O. Personal Writing Experiences	#23, #24
P. Listening to Oral Reading: How To	#3, #4
Q. Tips for Oral Reading	#3, #4
R. Ten Commitments for Parents	All

A. Family Reading Check-up

The following suggestions give you an opportunity to examine your current family reading practices with an eye toward adding more positive reading practices to your family's schedule. Begin by placing a check before each true statement. Then place a star by one unchecked item that you and your family would like to try to do. In a month or so, recheck all true statements. Hopefully, the starred item will then become one of the ones that you check.

Note: Check only those items that you do on a regular basis.

☐ 1. I read aloud to my child(ren).

☐ 2. I buy books for birthday and holiday gifts.

☐ 3. The family goes on brief trips beyond the neighborhood so that everyone is exposed to new experiences.

☐ 4. Family members make regular use of the library.

☐ 5. I praise my child(ren) for at least one improvement or accomplishment each day.

☐ 6. My child(ren) see(s) me reading for both pleasure and information from a variety of books, magazines, and newspapers.

☐ 7. My child(ren) know(s) that I take a positive interest in all of his/her/their school subjects.

☐ 8. I encourage my child(ren) to help select appropriate TV programs for family viewing.

☐ 9. I am an active and attentive listener and encourage my child(ren) to tell me about his/her/their daily experiences.

☐ 10. I make sure that my child(ren) is/are well-rested and has/have a good breakfast each day before school.

☐ 11. Our family plays word games and other learning activities.

☐ 12. My child(ren) has/have a dictionary that is appropriate for his/her/their age and ability.

☐ 13. My child(ren) has/have a bookcase or shelf in his/her/their room to keep and store personal books.

☐ 14. I encourage my child(ren) to write notes and letters and provide needed help when necessary.

☐ 15. I encourage my child(ren) to read for enjoyment every day.

B. Book Sharing Questions

In addition to the who, what, where, when, and why questions that could be asked about a story, you may want to select one or two of the following questions each time that you and your child share a book together.

1. If you were in the story, how would you feel?

2. If you were the author, how would you change the story?

3. If you were the main character, what would you do at the end of the story?

4. Was there anything special that you liked or did not like about the story? Tell me about it.

5. How would the story be different if the main character was someone else?

6. How would the story change if it took place where we live?

7. What other events could happen with the same character?

8. How would you act toward the main character if he/she was one of your friends?

C. Interest Inventory

Use this inventory to discover the kinds of things which your child(ren) would like to read. Either explain each appropriate item to a younger child and check his or her responses or let your child(ren) read each item and check those that he or she finds interesting. This process will assist you in determining stimulating reading material for your child(ren).

☐ 1. adventure
☐ 2. animals
☐ 3. antiques
☐ 4. art/music/dance
☐ 5. awards
☐ 6. careers
☐ 7. cars/motorcycles
☐ 8. cooking/food
☐ 9. exercise/health
☐ 10. famous people
☐ 11. fashion
☐ 12. foreign lands
☐ 13. games
☐ 14. houseplants
☐ 15. human body

☐ 16. insects
☐ 17. make-believe
☐ 18. miniatures/models
☐ 19. mysteries
☐ 20. old coins
☐ 21. painting/drawing
☐ 22. romance/love
☐ 23. self-defense
☐ 24. sewing/embroidery
☐ 25. science fiction
☐ 26. space
☐ 27. sports
☐ 28. stamps
☐ 29. trivia
☐ 30. world events

D. Lots of Things to Read

Books, magazines, and newspapers only scratch the surface of available reading materials for your children. The following list of other things to read was compiled from many sources, including kids.

signs	scoreboards	tombstones	tires
airplanes	grocery lists	bags	belts
bottles	catalogs	tools	glasses
shirts	aisle markers	checks	shoe boxes
door handles	place mats	ads	tattoos
money	birthday cakes	mailboxes	underwear
billboards	shower curtains	bumper stickers	stamps
trucks	price tags	buttons	posters
watches	timetables	trademarks	decorations
fire exits	itineraries	globes	songs
toys	kit instructions	game directions	light switches
stickers	food labels	toothpaste tubes	lawn mowers
bottle caps	buildings	brochures	calendars
stairs	name tags	fortune cookies	coupons
pajamas	paint cans	sugar packets	clocks
book covers	locks	historical signs	street names
letters	candy wrappers	engravings	decals
magnets	buses	legal documents	cue cards
wallets	pictures	vending machines	napkins
appliances	baseball bats	postmarks	restrooms
computers	elevators	postcards	erasers
license plates	menus	paintings	bills
tickets	wrist bands	pencils/pens	recipes
Band-aids	silverware	doors	marquees
cartons	crayons	light bulbs	cups
medicine labels	sheets	tennis shoes	plaques
patches	ties	fire alarms	calculators
credit cards	envelopes	boxes	maps
packages	jewelry	flags	record albums
schedules	poems	programs	toothbrushes

E. Words of Encouragement

Try these different ways to say that you are a proud parent. Let your child know that you are proud of his or her efforts.

That's really nice.

Wow!

That's great.

I like the way you did this.

Keep up the good work.

That's quite an improvement.

Much better.

Good job.

This kind of work pleases me.

Terrific.

Beautiful.

Congratulations.

You only missed a few.

Thanks for working so hard.

It looks like you put a lot of effort into this work.

Look how much better your (spelling, writing) looks.

Very creative.

Tell me how you did this.

I'm impressed.

Good answers.

Tell me how you chose your anwser.

Thank you for bringing home this good paper.

Good for you.

Now you've got the idea.

Exactly right.

Wonderful work.

That's a good point.

Nice going.

Let's hang this paper up.

Let's save this paper in a folder.

My, you have improved.

Let's send this to Grandma/pa.

Your work looks better every day.

I'm really proud of you for trying so hard.

F. Magazines for Children

A whole new world opens up to youngsters whose parents encourage them to subscribe to a children's magazine. The following list of such magazines include some children's favorites. Check with your librarian for current prices.

Child Life is a monthly magazine during the school year and bi-monthly during the summer. It is a mystery and science fiction magazine for ages 7-14.

> Saturday Evening Post Company
> P.O. 567-B
> 1100 Waterway Blvd.
> Indianapolis, IN 46202

Children's Digest is published monthly except in June and August. It contains old and new fiction, classic and contemporary authors, articles on science and history, book reviews, and activity pages. It is for ages 7-12.

> Parents Magazine Enterprises, Inc.
> 42 Vanderbilt Ave.
> New York, NY 10017

Children's Playmate is published monthly during the school year and bi-montly in the summer. It includes articles, fiction, activity pages, and reader contributions for ages 3-8.

> Saturday Evening Post Company
> P.O. Box 567-B
> 1100 Waterway Blvd.
> Indianapolis, IN 46202

Cricket is a monthly literature magazine for ages 6-12. It includes stories, articles, and poems by internationally known writers as well as activity pages, crafts, and reader contributions.

> Open Court Publishing Company
> Box 599
> LaSalle, IL 61301

Highlights for Children is published eleven times a year. It is geared toward fostering creativity in children ages 3-12. It includes biographies, elementary social studies, literature, and science material as well as activity pages.

> Highlights for Children, Inc.
> P.O. Box 269
> 2300 West Fifth Ave.
> Columbus, OH 43216

Humpty Dumpty's Magazine is a monthly magazine for ages 3-7. It contains stories and features which entertain as well as develop vocabulary and reading skills.

> Parents Magazine Enteprises, Inc.
> 52 Vanderbilt Ave.
> New York, NY 10017

Jack and Jill is a monthly magazine for ages 5-12. It contains a variety of stories and articles on different reading levels as well as activities and crafts.

> Jack and Jill Publishing Company
> 1100 Waterway Blvd.
> Indianapolis, IN 46202

G. Listening Checklist

Each member of the family will find this checklist useful. Check the most appropriate response for each question. Try it again in a month to see if your listening has improved.

	Never	Sometimes	Always
1. Do I look directly at the speaker?	☐	☐	☐
2. If the speaker is close to me, do I look him/her directly in the eyes?	☐	☐	☐
3. Do I concentrate on the speaker instead of waiting for my turn to speak?	☐	☐	☐
4. Do I avoid interrupting the speaker at mid-thought?	☐	☐	☐
5. Am I able to follow verbal directions the first time?	☐	☐	☐
6. Do I listen courteously to children as well as adults?	☐	☐	☐

H. Reading with Your Child: Five Easy Steps

1. **Select a book.** Either have your child select his or her own book or you select one based on a topic that you know will be interesting to the child. (Don't guess. Ask your child!)
   a. If the book is much too easy, let your child tape record parts of it to build fluency and confidence.
   b. If your child is a reluctant reader, alternate reading sentences or paragraphs with him or her.
   c. If the book is much too difficult, you read it aloud and let your child talk about the pictures or summarize sections that you read.

2. **Have your child read aloud.** Sometimes just part of a story is sufficient. Allow the child to choose the part with the "action" or one with a good description, etc.
   a. Have him or her read to you, your spouse, younger brothers and sisters, the neighbors, even to pets.
   b. Try sending a taped read-along story to grandparents or a favorite relative or friend.
   c. Just be a good listener as your child reads. Try to comment positively on just part of the story to let your child know that you were paying attention.

3. **Simply tell your child any unknown words he or she encounters.** Stopping to use a dictionary will interrupt the thread of the story especially if he or she is usually reluctant to read.

   a. Later on, you might go back to the word and demonstrate that using the other words in the sentence plus the first letter of the word can give him or her a good clue.
   b. At all costs, refrain from making negative comments about how easy the word was or that he or she should have known it, etc.

4. **Discuss the story.** Try to make both reading the story and discussing it enjoyable experiences.
   a. Try not to ask too many questions!
   b. Ask some questions which require more than just a "yes" or "no" answer.
   c. Include opinion questions as a way to spark creativity.
      Sample: How would you change the ending?

5. **Praise your child.** Reading should be enjoyable for both of you. Sometimes a sincere "thank you for reading to me" along with a smile or a hug will be the best praise for the situation.
   a. Find ways to praise honestly and sincerely.
   b. Praise improvement as well as good performance.
   c. Try praising your child for being attentive, using expression, using correct pronunciation, or for selecting an interesting story.

I. Using Games

Reinforcement is necessary to insure that learning takes place. Games provide a pleasant atmosphere for children to enjoy themselves and practice reading skills at the same time. Competition should be geared to self-improvement goals rather than to determining a winner.

SIGHT VOCABULARY

Sight word games are quite popular. Sight words are words that your child recognizes instantly without analysis. The larger the store of sight words, the more quickly and fluently a child is able to read. Words for sight word games can be taken from papers your child brings home from school, from household items, from schoolbooks, or from teacher-made lists. Try some of these games.

1. **Fish Pond.** Write words on cards cut in the shape of a fish. Attach a paper clip to the mouth of each fish. Use a small magnet tied to a string to "fish" words out of a bowl. Have your child say the word he or she "catches."

2. **Hide The Word.** Write words on several word cards. Place the cards face up on the floor or table. Have your child study the words for about thirty seconds and then cover his or her eyes. Remove one card. Have your child determine the missing word.

3. **Save Pack.** Print the words on word cards and quickly flash the cards to your child. If he or she misses a word, it is put in a "save pack." After he or she has studied the words in the "save pack," he or she plays the game again. The goal is to have an empty "save pack."

4. **Spin the Platter.** Use a large paper plate or a piece of cardboard from the pizza parlor. Attach an arrow with a brass paper fastener to the center of the circle. Print words in pencil around the edge of the circle. Have your child spin the arrow and identify the word it touches. If correct, your child gets a point.

5. **Clue.** Print some words on word cards. Put them face up on the floor or on a table. The first player gives a clue about one of the words, such as it begins the same way that "dog" does. If the next player guesses the word correctly, it is his or her turn to give the next clue. If the next player can not guess corectly, another player tries his or her skill.

Other Skills: Educational games can reinforce phonetic analysis, structural analysis, vocabulary, and comprehension skills. The particular format shown below, for instance, can be adapted to any category and thus reinforce many skills.

Try Your Skill: On the left side of the box, list some letters of the alphabet. Across the top, list your categories. For example, if you are interested in reinforcing some vocabulary, you might use the following letters and categories.

Try Your Skill/Vocabulary			
	homonyms	antonyms	synonyms
r	right write	right wrong	right correct
s	so sew	sad happy	see look
t	to two too	top bottom	tip edge
h	here hear	hot cold	help aid

Another example: phonetic analysis

Try Your Skill/Long Vowel Sounds					
	a	e	i	o	u
t	tape	team	tie	toe	tube
r	rate	real	rise	rose	rule
m	make	meet	mile	most	mule
p	pace	peel	pile	pole	pew*

*Remember that the skill was vowel sounds, not vowel letters!

Try Your Skill can also be used to study for social studies, science, and math. All you need to do is choose the categories that fit the need.

J. Travel Games

Traveling with children sometimes becomes a problem. Occupying them so that they are less aware of the change in schedule often makes getting to and from the destination more enjoyable for all. Try some of these games on the next trip you take.

1. **I'm Going to Mary's.** The first person begins by saying, "I'm going to Mary's and I'm taking some **milk**." The next player repeats that sentence replacing "milk" with another word that begins with "m." Older children might repeat "milk" and then add another word beginning with "m." Continue until no one can think of another word. Then work with another consonant.

2. **Magic Word.** Before the trip, everyone agrees on the magic word. During the trip as people are talking, everyone listens for the "magic word." The first one to raise his or her hand when the word is heard gets a point. At the end of the trip, give a treat to the person with the most points.

3. **License Plate Identification.** This game has a variety of options. Use whichever appeals to your child.
   a. Write the first ten license plate letters you see. See who can alphabetize the list correctly.
   b. Have a list of states for each person. See who can identify the most out-of-town license plates on a trip. Reuse the same lists to see who can find plates for all the states.
   c. Have everyone write the first two license plates that have numbers on them. Rearrange them quickly and then add, subtract, multiply, or divide them.

4. **Buying Game.** One person begins by saying, "I'm going to (place beginning with an "a") to buy (an item beginning with an "a"). The second person repeats the sentence and adds a place and item with a "b." See if the family can get all the way to "z." Help younger children by working in pairs.

5. **Diary.** Have your child keep a diary of dates and places visited.

6. **Following Routes.** As you travel, let your child follow the route on the map and help direct the driver to the final destination.

7. **I See Something.** Begin by saying, "I see something that begins with a "b." Whoever identifies the object as a "barn" or "bottle" etc. thinks up the next riddle. Vary the clues to include rhyming words, word meaning etc.

8. **Categories.** Have your child classify objects and activities. Have him or her name all the fruits or vegetables he or she can, then furniture, animals, toys, etc. Then move to school activities, sports, quiet games etc.

9. **Storytelling.** Have one person tell another a favorite story.

K. Comprehension Tips

The following procedure is designed to help your child become more actively involved in the stories he or she reads. Once children are actively involved, they can understand or comprehend more of what they read. You can encourage your child to become an active reader at home by following these steps:

1. Ask your child to choose an interesting book or story. Have some paper and a pencil to write questions.

2. Have your child read the title of the story or book. Ask your child to think of questions that he or she would like to ask about the title. Write those on the paper.

3. Have your child look through the pictures and illustrations and ask questions about them. Write those on the paper.

4. Have your child read the story silently or listen to you read it aloud. Ask your child to stop you every so often to ask more questions to add to the list.

5. As you or your child continues the story, remind him or her to be alert for the answers to the questions as the story continues.

6. After the story is complete, discuss the questions and answers together. Go back to the story to find answers that can not be remembered.

7. Talk about any questions that could not be answered.

8. Follow-up the story with a creative question of your own such as: "What would have happened if...?" or "Why do you think...?"

L. Suggestions for Improving Comprehension

1. Help your child set a purpose for reading by asking a question before reading the selection.

2. After reading, have your child summarize the important ideas either verbally or in writing. Discuss why some ideas are included while others are not.

3. After reading, ask your child to write a main idea statement or a new title for the story. Then write at least three supporting details.

4. Use the **SQ3R Method** to read or study factual material.
   a. **S**urvey: read only the headlines, captions, and summaries.
   b. **Q**uestion: ask Who, What, Where, When, and Why questions about what you surveyed.
   c. **R**ead: read to find the answers to your questions.
   d. **R**ecite: write and study the answers to your questions.
   e. **R**eview: reexamine all your notes.

5. Ask your child to look at questions at the end of the story before reading the story.

6. Have your child read a story then make up test questions about it. Have him or her take the test or give it to you to take.

7. Have your child keep a notebook of vocabulary words along with their definitions and how they are used in sentences. You may want to go over this notebook with your child every once in a while.

M. Resources for Parents

The following list contains suggestions to assist you as you become an active partner in your child's education. Please check with your librarian for other available materials.

Kaye, Peggy. *Games for Reading: Playful Ways to Help Your Child Read*. New York: Pantheon Books, 1984.

Larrick, Nancy. *A Parent's Guide to Children's Reading*. (5th ed.) New York: Bantam Books, 1982.

Fredericks, Anthony. *Raising Bookworms: A Parent's Guide to Reading Success*. Saratoga, CA: R & E Publishers, 1985.

Lamme, Linda Leonard. *Growing Up Reading*. Washington, D.C., Acropolis Books, Ltd., 1985.

Hearne, Betsy. *Choosing Books for Children: A Common Sense Guide*. New York: Delacorte Press, 1981.

Smethurst, Wood. *Teaching Your Children to Read at Home*. New York: McGraw-Hill Publishing Company, 1975.

Trelease, Jim. *The Read-Aloud Handbook*. New York: Penguin Books, 1985.

Lamme, Linda Leonard. *Growing Up Writing*. Washington, D.C., Acropolis Books, Ltd., 1984.

N. Tuning in to Reading and Television

The following suggestions will help your child appreciate both reading and television as well as the place each has in life.

1. Encourage your child to read about a favorite subject after watching a program about it. You can help by noticing special interests and giving him or her books about it.

2. Discuss programs your child watches to determine what is fantasy and what is reality, what is true or untrue, and what is real or unreal.

3. Encourage your child to write to television personalities and networks offering praise or complaints or asking questions.

4. Suggest that your child look for articles about television programs and stars in the newspapers.

5. Encourage your child to study the weekly television schedule. Each family member might select an evening's family viewing.

6. Join your child in watching some of his or her favorite programs. Bring up cause and effect by asking, "Why did he or she do that?" or "What will happen next?"

7. Give the television a day off. Have a family read-a-thon instead.

8. Suggest that your child use a T.V. listing and a calendar to develop a weekly family viewing schedule. Encourage your child to plan one hour of reading for each hour of T.V.

O. Personal Writing Experiences

Writing is an important part of everyday life. You can help your child become a better reader and writer by following some of these suggestions.

1. After your child draws a picture, have him or her tell you about it so you can write one or two sentences below it.

2. Consider mailing pictures with descriptions to friends or relatives. Show your child how to address the envelope.

3. Encourage your child to write "thank you" notes for gifts or watch as you write what he or she says.

4. Help your child keep a journal. Fasten lined paper together by tieing yarn through the holes. Ask your child what happened that day and record his or her exact words. Each week review the material. As your child becomes better at writing, turn the writing over to him or her but continue the sharing.

5. Older children like keeping a diary—a natural outcome of keeping a journal. Be sure that a child's diary remains personal. Do not read it without permission.

6. Have your child write a book of definitions such as "Loneliness is...", "Imagination..." complete with pictures.

7. Keep a special book or folder for unusual happenings. Either pictures or words can be used. Share this with the family.

8. Try to tickle your child's funny bone by having him or her rewrite familiar stories with amusing word changes. Share these during family time.

From *Letters to Parents,* Copyright © 1986 Scott, Foresman and Company

P. Listening to Oral Reading: How To

The following tips will help both parent and child enjoy the experience of the child reading to the parent.

1. Establish a relaxed atmosphere.

2. Use a variety of easy reading material.

3. Be sensitive to your child's interests.

4. Have your child choose the material to be read.

5. Be a reassuring and supportive listener.

6. Remember that the meaning of what is read is much more important than reading the exact words. Ignore:
   a. meaningful substitutions such as "tiny, little cat" instead of "small, little cat."
   b. omitting an insignificant word that does not change the meaning such as "told what he heard" instead of "told what he had heard."
   c. word order changes that do not affect meaning such as "put the tent up" instead of "put up the tent."
   d. addition of words that do not change meaning such as "the little old man" instead of "the old man."

7. Be aware that most people understand more when reading silently than when reading orally. Provide your child with opportunities to read a selection silently before reading it aloud.

Q. Tips for Oral Reading

When your child reads aloud, always remember that one necessary ingredient is your attention. Listen while your child reads. Try not to become another teacher. Here are some other tips.

1. Have your child read only parts of a story to you such as the humorous parts or any dialogue.

2. Take turns reading alternate paragraphs with your child.

3. Have your child practice by reading into a tape recorder and listening to himself or herself afterwards. This is a great confidence builder.

4. Read aloud to your child. Make intentional mistakes and see if he or she can detect them. Be obvious at first.

5. Before reading a story, tell your child to listen very carefully because you are going to stop before the end. When you stop, ask your child to finish the story with a possible ending. Don't forget to read ahead first to find a good stopping point.

6. Keep a family calendar. Have your child read the daily entries.

7. Encourage your child to read the menu when the family eats out.

8. Have your child read aloud the directions to a new game.

9. Let your child read aloud road signs on a short trip.

10. Encourage your child to read aloud television program descriptions before he or she selects a program.

R. Ten Commitments for Parents

1. I will read with my child(ren) on a daily basis.

2. I will provide my child(ren) with a quiet, comfortable place to read and study.

3. I will encourage my child(ren) to develop a personal library and will contribute to it regularly.

4. I will provide my child(ren) with a wide range of experiences.

5. I will talk with (not to) my child(ren) on a daily basis.

6. I will praise my child(ren) for at least one success or improvement each day.

7. I will hug my child(ren) at least once a day.

8. I will respect each child as an individual — each with his or her unique talents and abilities.

9. I will provide family activities which encourage my child(ren) to grow in mind, soul, and body.

10. I will encourage my child(ren) to view reading as an enjoyable and fulfilling lifetime experience.

Family Reading Award

This Certificate is Hereby
Presented to the Family of

_____

For Participating in ____ or More Weeks
of Fun Reading Activities.

SUPER READER

_____
Teacher

_____
Date

_____
School

_____
Principal